To _____

From _____

Growing older
Is like slowly going up in an airplane.
The horizon gets wider and wider
As we look down on the earth,
And things become smaller and smaller
And of much less importance
In the panoramic view
Of our soul.

The Helen Steiner Rice Foundation

When someone does a kindness
it always seems to me
That's the way God up in heaven
would like us all to be . . .

Whatever the celebration, whatever the day, whatever the event, whatever the occasion, Helen Steiner Rice possessed the ability to express the appropriate feeling for that particular moment. A happening became happier, a sentiment more sentimental, a memory more memorable because of her deep sensitivity and ability to put into understandable language the emotion being experienced. Her positive attitude, her concern for others, and her love of God are identifiable threads woven into her life, her work . . . and even her death.

Prior to Mrs. Rice's passing, she established the HELEN STEINER RICE FOUNDATION, a nonprofit corporation that awards grants to worthy charitable programs assisting the elderly and the needy.

Royalties from the sale of this book will add to the financial capabilities of the HELEN STEINER RICE FOUNDATION. Because of limited resources, the foundation presently limits grants to qualified charitable programs in Lorain, Ohio, where Helen Steiner Rice was born, and Greater Cincinnati, Ohio, where Mrs. Rice lived and worked most of her life. Hopefully in the future, resources will be of sufficient size that broader geographical areas may be considered in the awarding of grants.

Because of her foresight, caring, and deep conviction of sharing, Helen Steiner Rice continues to touch a countless number of lives through foundation grants and through her inspirational poetry.

Thank you for your assistance in helping to keep Helen's dream alive and growing.

Andrea Cornett, Administrator

Celebrating the Golden Years

Merry Christmas Dolores! 2017

Helen Steiner Rice

and

Virginia J. Ruehlmann

I came across this book, the same very day we spoke on the phone, & I thought it was perfect! Hope to visit in 2018!

Enjoy!

Love, Kathy

Fleming H. Revell
A Division of Baker Book House
Grand Rapids, Michigan 49516

Published by Fleming H. Revell
a division of Baker Book House Company
P.O. Box 6287, Grand Rapids, MI 49516-6287

Printed in the United States of America

Library of Congress Cataloging-in-Publication Data

Rice, Helen Steiner.
    Celebrating the golden years / Helen Steiner Rice and Virginia J.
Ruehlmann.
      p. cm.
    ISBN 0-8007-1749-X
      1. Christian poetry, American. 2. Aging—Poetry. I. Ruehlmann,
Virginia J. II. Title.
    [PS3568.I28G66 1998]
    811'.54—dc21   98-4920

Jacket and interior paintings by Michael Ingle

Scripture quotations identified NIV are from the HOLY BIBLE, NEW INTERNA-
TIONAL VERSION®. NIV®. Copyright © 1973, 1978, 1984 by International Bible Society. Used by permission of Zondervan Publishing House. All rights reserved.

Scripture quotations identified RSV are from the Revised Standard Version of the Bible,
copyright 1946, 1952, 1971 by the Division of Christian Education of the National
Council of the Churches of Christ in the USA. Used by permission.

To
all present golden agers—
grandparents, retirees, senior citizens—
all future ones,
and all former ones
who provided the example
of how to add years gracefully
while remaining young in spirit,
positive in attitude,
firm in faith,
and maintaining a zest for living

Contents

Introduction

Headlines inform us that our nation is "graying." Articles and statistics indicate that men and women are living longer than their grandparents and are remaining more productive in later life. Our society as a whole is growing older. What does it mean to grow old? Is it determined by the number of years a person has lived? Does it take place when one retires from employment, enters a retirement home, or becomes a grandparent?

Growing old is an attitude that does not hinge on one's age, marital status, health, or employment. A person can celebrate a ninetieth birthday and remain young in spirit. A person's perspective determines whether one is growing old. An individual's outlook on life depends on sustaining an abiding faith, maintaining family bonds, preserving present friendships and developing new ones, staying as fit and active as possible, remembering the past but looking forward to the future, retaining a good sense of humor, celebrating life, reaching out to others, and keeping a zest for living. These are the very actions and techniques advocated by Helen Steiner Rice in her poetry and her recommendations for everyday living.

Mrs. Rice recognized the importance of practicing what she preached in her poems. Despite suffering physical challenges and hardships in her later years, she maintained a positive perspective and viewed aging as a season in one's life. She wrote that various cycles of life are sent by God, and each season of life should be accepted as such and enjoyed as much as possible.

May the words of Helen Steiner Rice and her example inspire you to appreciate each happening, enjoy each opportunity, face each challenge, and accept gracefully and gratefully each season of life that comes to you.

Reaching senior citizen status is a precious accomplishment. It is an achievement of which one can be justifiably proud. It is a grand, glorious, and golden time of life. Enjoy and value it!

Gloriously,
Virginia J. Ruehlmann

Faith and Prayers

Life would not be worth living without faith. Faith in God; faith in ourselves; faith in our fellow-men; we should omit none of the three. Without faith in God, there is no hope for the soul; without faith in self, life is a miserable failure; without faith in each other, we should miss the sweet joys of friendship. Keep your faith bright; let its luster never grow dim!

Ida Scott Taylor

- Thank God every day for your blessings.
- Offer prayers for other individuals.
- Share your love for God.
- Apply your faith in everyday happenings.
- Trust God always.

Good Morning, God

You are ushering in another day,
    untouched and freshly new,
So here I am to ask You, God,
    if You'll renew me too.
Forgive the many errors
    that I made yesterday
And let me try again, dear God,
    to walk closer in Your way.
But, Father, I am well aware
    I can't make it on my own,
So take my hand and hold it tight,
    for I can't walk alone.

Blessed are all who fear the LORD,
who walk in his ways.

Psalm 128:1 NIV

A Prayer for Patience

God, teach me to be patient,
  teach me to go slow—
Teach me how to wait on You
  when my way I do not know.
Teach me sweet forbearance
  when things do not go right,
So I remain unruffled
  when others grow uptight.
Teach me how to quiet
  my racing, rising heart,
So I may hear the answer
  You are trying to impart.
Teach me to let go, dear God,
  and pray undisturbed until
My heart is filled with inner peace
  and I learn to know Your will.

You can preach a better sermon with your life than with your lips.

Oliver Goldsmith

Daily Prayers Are Heaven's Stairs

The stairway rises heaven-high,
  the steps are dark and steep.
In weariness we climb them
  as we stumble, fall, and weep.
And many times we falter
  along the path of prayer,
Wondering if You hear us
  and if You really care.
Oh, give us some assurance,
  restore our faith anew,
So we can keep on climbing
  the stairs of prayer to You.
For we are weak and wavering,
  uncertain and unsure,
And only meeting You in prayer
  can help us to endure
All life's trials and troubles,
  its sickness, pain, and sorrow,
And give us strength and courage
  to face and meet tomorrow.

Pray till prayer makes you forget your own wish, and leave
it or merge it in God's will.

Frederick W. Robertson

Daily Prayers
Dissolve Your Cares

I meet God in the morning
  and go with Him through the day,
Then in the stillness of the night
  before sleep comes I pray
That God will just take over
  all the problems I couldn't solve,
And in the peacefulness of sleep
  my cares will all dissolve,
So when I open up my eyes
  to greet another day,
I'll find myself renewed in strength
  and there will open up a way
To meet what seemed impossible
  for me to solve alone,
And once again I'll be assured
  I am never on my own.

Thou dost keep him in perfect peace,
whose mind is stayed on thee,
because he trusts in thee.

Isaiah 26:3 RSV

A Special Thank-You

Thank You, God, for everything
   I've experienced here on earth.
Thank You for protecting me
   from the hour of my birth.
Thank You, God, for little things
   that often come my way—
The unexpected little joys
   that brighten up my day.
And thank You for the beauty
   around me everywhere—
The gentle rain and glistening dew,
   the sunshine and the air,
The joyous gift of feeling
   the soul's soft, whispering voice
That speaks to me from deep within
   and makes my heart rejoice.

Oh, God, no words are great enough
   to thank You just for living,
And that is why each day
   is a day for real thanksgiving.

A truly happy old age is the result not made of work or
play; it is possible only for individuals who have learned
from infancy that by making the most of immediate life,
they are preparing themselves for a continuously active
and productive life.

Agnes E. Meyer

He Loves You

It's amazing and incredible,
   but it's as true as it can be—
God loves and understands us all,
   and that means you and me.
His grace is all sufficient
   for both the young and old,
For the lonely and the timid,
   for the brash and for the bold.
His love knows no exceptions,
   so never feel excluded—
No matter who or what you are,
   your name has been included.

And no matter what your past has been,
   trust God to understand,
And no matter what your problem is,
   just place it in His hand,
For in all of our unloveliness
   this great God loves us still—
He loved us since the world began
   and what's more, He always will!

As you grow older, more than ever before, you need to spend part of each day alone in peace, quiet, and meditation; and in prayer that you may be shown how to continue to live each day with courage, kindness, wisdom, laughter, interest, and understanding.

William B. Terhune

Family Affection

The beauty of a home is harmony.
The security of a home is loyalty.
The joy of a home is love.
The plenty of a home is in children.
The rule of a home is service.
The comfort of a home is in contented spirits.
The maker of a home, of a real human home, is God Himself,
the same Who made the stars and built the world.

Frank Crane

- The home must radiate love, honesty, respect, and belief in God.
- Stay in touch with all members of your family.
- Create memorable moments that will become lasting, loving memories.
- View old photograph albums, family movies, or videos.
- Read a story to a child or share one of your talents.
- Frequently offer words of encouragement and praise.
- God has a specific plan for children and senior citizens. He created them for each other to share time and love. If you have no grandchildren, volunteer for an intergenerational project or become a foster grandparent.

God Bless Your Anniversary

This happy anniversary proves
   a fact you can't disparage—
It takes true love and faith and hope
   to make a happy marriage.
And it takes a lot of praying
   and a devoted man and wife
To keep God ever present
   in their home and in their life.

Though I am growing old, I maintain that the best is yet
to come—the time when one may see things more dis-
passionately and know oneself and others more truly, and
perhaps be able to do more, and in religion rest centered
in a few simple truths.

Benjamin Jowett

Express Your Love to Your Son

There are so many things that my heart wants to say,
But there are no words big enough to convey
The things I feel about you, my son,
And all of the wonderful things you have done
To lighten my burdens and brighten my days
And make life worth living in so many ways.
For all the things that are sad and distressing
Through you I am able to accept as a blessing,
For God blessed my life when He gave me you,
And God truly loves you and I love you too.
And if you could look into my heart today,
You would know what your mother would like to say,
For a mother's love expresses so well
The depth of love that I cannot tell.
But I want you to know, dear son of mine,
That no love except the love that's divine
Could ever exceed my love for you
And my thanks for the wonderful things you do.

How we think shows through in how we act. Attitudes are
mirrors of the mind. They reflect thinking.

David Joseph Schwartz

A Mother's Love

A mother's love is like an island
   in life's ocean vast and wide—
A peaceful, quiet shelter
   from the restless, rising tide.
A mother's love is like a fortress,
   and we seek protection there
When the waves of tribulation
   seem to drown us in despair.
A mother's love is a sanctuary
   where our souls can find sweet rest
From the struggle and the tension
   of life's fast and futile quest.
A mother's love is like a tower
   rising far above the crowd,
And her smile is like the sunshine
   breaking through a threatening cloud.
A mother's love is like a beacon
   burning bright with faith and prayer,
And through the changing scenes of life
   we can find a haven there . . .

For a mother's love is fashioned
after God's enduring love—
It is endless and unfailing
like the love of God above.

Love bears all things, believes all things, hopes all things,
endures all things.

1 Corinthians 13:7 RSV

A Tribute to Daughters

Every home should have a daughter,
    for there's nothing like a girl
To keep the world around her
    in one continuous whirl.
She is soft and sweet and cuddly,
    but she's also wise and smart—
She's a wondrous combination
    of mind and brain and heart.
She starts out as a rosebud—
    her petals softly sealed—
And as she grows she blossoms
    with a lovely soul revealed.

Little girls are the nicest things that happen to people.
They are born with a little bit of angel-shine about them,
and though it wears thin sometimes, there is always
enough left to lasso your heart—even when they are sit-
ting in the mud, or crying temperamental tears, or parad-
ing up the street in Mother's best clothes.

Alan Beck

Grandpa

God, grant me this, I humbly pray,
May I so live from day to day
That I will be more worthy of
The kindness and the thoughtful love
That my dear children give to me,
And to be the man their children see,
When they look up and say sincerely,
"Grandpa, we love you so very dearly."
And may I somehow in some way
So live and speak from day to day
That I'm the man at least in part
My family treasures in their heart.

Not what we give, but what we share, for the gift without
the giver is bare.

James Russell Lowell

Fellowship of Friends

In youth, every chance-met acquaintance is hailed as a friend. But as one grows older, and the real nature of friendship becomes better understood, fewer and fewer wear for one the golden name of friend. For the man or woman who has reached the middle life with half a dozen friends, real friends who will bear all the tests of friendship, is rarely fortunate. One or two such friends are all that most of us can hope to win, and we may count ourselves rich with them.

Author Unknown

- Friendships are gifts—treasure yours.
- Extend unconditional love to a hurting individual.
- Say a kind word. Share a smile. Send a letter. Lend a listening ear. An act of kindness means so much.
- Include a lonely person in a holiday celebration.
- A cup of tea or glass of lemonade takes on new meaning when shared.
- Pick a bouquet of lilacs or a single rose for a neighbor.
- Give away a hug. A hug contains no calories, no cholesterol, no fat, no artificial ingredients, and is easily returnable.

The Golden Chain of Friendship

Friendship is a golden chain—
　　the links are friends so dear—
Growing just a bit more lovely
　　with every passing year.
It's clasped together firmly
　　with a love that's deep and true,
And it's rich with happy memories
　　and glad recollections too.
Time can't destroy its beauty,
　　for as long as memory lives,
Years can't erase the pleasure
　　that the joy of friendship gives.

Blessed is the person who has the gift of making friends,
for it is one of God's best gifts. It involves many things,
but above all the power of going outside of one's self, and
seeing and appreciating whatever is noble and loving in
another person.

Thomas Hughes

The Help of a Friend

As the years go hurrying by,
　　I pause and think anew
How fortunate I was to meet
　　a kind, wise friend like you.
And I am but one of many
　　who owe a lot to you,
For all the help you've given,
　　and time and effort too.
And this is just a welcome chance
　　to tell you that you've won
The real success in life
　　for the fine things you have done.

It gives me great pleasure to converse with the aged. They have been over the road that all must travel, and know where it is rough and difficult and where it is level and easy.

Plato

Folks like You

It's folks like you we like to meet,
We like to see, we like to greet.
We like to talk and have them near
Because they bring good will and cheer
And leave a pleasant memory too
Whenever they are gone from you.

It's folks like you the whole world needs,
Who brighten living with kindly deeds.
It's folks like you, who lay no claim
To what the world accepts as fame,
Who are the folks who really rate
The honors of the truly great,
For what is greater than to be
Beloved by everyone you see?

Youth is the age to receive instruction, middle age to make
use of it, and old age to impart it to others.

Pythagoras

33

Your Letter

The days go by and as they do
I often pause to think of you.
And while I know that it is true
That I don't tell you that I do,
It's just because I don't have time
To stop and dash you off a rhyme.

In this world of restlessness
We should take time for happiness,
But little promptings of the heart
Are stilled before they get a start.
But please believe I think of you
And very, very often too.

I want you to know that you made my heart sing.
Your letter was truly a beautiful thing.
And the reason it touched me is perfectly clear—
Your message was simple, so sweet and sincere.
And of the many nice things that I can recall,
Your letter was one of the nicest of all.

The constant interchange of those thousand little courtesies which imperceptibly sweeten life has a happy effect upon the features and spreads a mellow evening charm over the wrinkles of age.

Washington Irving

Thoughts of You

The years bring many changes
   in many ways, it's true,
But one thing never changes
   and that's my thoughts of you.
I remember you distinctly,
   not just a pretty face,
For beauty is just something
   that the passing years erase.
But you have something
   that glistens from within,
For your beauty, my friend,
   is much deeper than the skin.
And that is why I think of you
   and remember you with pride,
For you are one of those rare people
   who is beautiful inside.

As a countenance is made beautiful by the soul shining
through it, so the world is beautiful by the shining through
it of God.

Friedrich Heinrich Jacobi

Everyone Needs Someone

People need people
  and friends need friends,
And we all need love,
  for a full life depends
Not on vast riches
  or great acclaim,
Not on success
  or worldly fame,
But on just knowing
  that someone cares
And holds us close
  in their thoughts and prayers,
For only the knowledge
  that we're understood
Makes everyday living
  feel wonderfully good.

Life is not a holiday, but an education. And the one eternal lesson for us all is how better to love.

Henry Drummond

Fit and Active Living

Experts in the field of gerontology substitute the words "change of occupation" for the word "retirement." This recognizes the fact that individuals are not made for inactivity. Observers who have watched what happens to active people when they "retire" with no new responsibilities or obligations have been appalled at the changes that this produces in their health, attitudes, and their spiritual responses.

John Park Lee

- Stay spiritually, physically, mentally, and socially active.
- Have regular physical, vision, dental, and hearing checkups.
- Store all prescribed medications in the original bottle.
- Always turn on the light when taking medicine at night.
- Observe the expiration date on all medications and dispose of expired ones in a proper and safe manner.
- Drink at least six eight-ounce glasses of water daily. Eat well-balanced meals including plenty of fruits, vegetables, and grains.
- Exercise daily, even if in a limited way.
- Take a walk, briskly if possible, otherwise at your own comfortable pace.
- Enroll in a class on a topic of interest to you: joy through movement, line or square dancing, water aerobics, art appreciation, painting, gardening.
- Plan a trip to a location you have always wanted to visit.
- Play card games and board games and fix puzzles. You will have fun, eliminate boredom, and maintain mental acuity and finger dexterity.
- Volunteer for the political party of your choice.

For Whom Do You Work?

I work for God and I work for His glory,
In all that I do, I retell the old story—
The story of life and how we should live,
How we should share and continually give.

Live your life while you have it. Life is a splendid gift.
There is nothing small in it. For the greatest things grow
by God's law out of the smallest. But to live your life you
must discipline it. You must not fritter it away. . . . But
make your thoughts, your acts, all work to the same end,
not self—but God. That is what we call Character.

Florence Nightingale

Our Strength

When our spiritual muscles get flabby
   and begin to waste away,
Then our morals are in danger
   and we become easy prey
For all the temptations
   that daily lurk near
And we find our morals cracking
   like a thin veneer.
And with self-indulgence
   we pave the way
To spiritual softness
   that leads us astray.

O Lord, Thou givest us everything at the price of an effort.

Leonardo da Vinci

You Grow Dearer
Every Year

Some folks grow older
   with birthdays, it's true,
But others grow nicer
   as years widen their view.
For years only add
   a bright inner charm,
And one year more or less
   is no cause for alarm,
For goodness and kindness
   add beauty and grace
That shine from the spirit
   and illuminate the face.
And a heart that is young
   lends an aura of grace
That rivals in beauty
   a young, pretty face.
For no one would notice
   a few little wrinkles
When a kind loving heart
   fills the eyes full of twinkles.

So don't count your years
   by the birthdays you've had,
But by the things you have done
   to make other folks glad.

The best cosmetic in the world is an active mind that is always finding something new.

Mary Meek Atkeson

Life

You'd be surprised if you only knew
How many letters I've started to you,
But somehow none of them ever got finished
For the flow of my words has greatly diminished,
And somehow I felt that to try and explain
Would be like trying to stop the onset of rain.
I knew I would find you most sympathetic
If I mentioned that I felt non-energetic.
You'd feel that you should reach out a helping hand
And try in some manner to understand,
But frankly sometimes I think it's God's will
That our minds seem frozen and life stands still,
And there comes a time we must slacken our pace
And accept the fact that we can't run every race.

So don't think my silence is just neglect
Or a sign of lost interest and admiring respect.
My zeal for your work is unchanged and unbroken,
It's just my words that remain unspoken.
Now don't think I don't find this hard to admit,
And for months I've been shying away from it,
I'd love to be eager and bursting with zeal,
The way I used to abundantly feel.
I've had physical checks and doctors attend me,
But only the Great Physician can mend me,
And whatever is happening inside of me
I'm sure it is just what's supposed to be.

Don't let the fact that you can't do all you want to do, keep
you from doing what you can do.

Francois de Salignac de La Mothe Fen'elon

Think Positively

I was shocked and surprised and filled with regret
To learn of your nasty spill and upset.
We sure never know what the day will bring,
And this is surely a very good thing,
For if we knew, we'd be filled with dread
Thinking of things that might be ahead.
But accidents happen all of the time
As you will see from this little rhyme.

Stars fall down from distant skies,
Black-eyed Susans get black eyes,
Pies get cut and pretzels get bent,
Eggs get beaten and dough gets spent.
So take it easy, don't fuss, fret, and stew,
Your accident was part of the pattern for you.
You may not understand, but it was probably best,
So make the most of your unwanted rest.

Positive thinking is reacting positively to a negative situation.

Bill Havens

Favorable Attitudes

Our Father, when we long for life without trials and work without difficulties, remind us that oaks grow strong in contrary winds and diamonds are made under pressure. With stout hearts may we see in every calamity an opportunity and not give way to the pessimist who sees in every opportunity a calamity.

Peter Marshall

- Concentrate on the positives in your life rather than the negatives.
- Look for the best in people.
- Believe in yourself.
- Share your talents.
- Adapt to and accept the challenges and changes that come with aging. Make the most of life every day.
- Precious metals, tapestries, and wine improve with age. So can you.
- Share a smile and laugh often. A good laugh helps you cope with stressful events.
- Maintain a strong sense of humor. Humor helps release tensions and diminishes anger.
- Improve your posture. How you carry yourself affects your attitude and how others perceive you.
- Participate in an intergenerational project. Your wisdom and experience plus the enthusiasm and energy of youth can create wonderful moments for all involved.
- Enroll in a driving refresher course for mature adults. You will enhance your knowledge, hone your skills, and maybe even help prevent a traffic accident.

This Too Will Pass Away

If I can endure for this minute
  whatever is happening to me,
No matter how heavy my heart is
  or how dark the moment might be,

If I can remain calm and quiet
    with all my world crashing about me,
Secure in the knowledge God loves me
    when everyone else seems to doubt me,
If I can but keep on believing
    what I know in my heart to be true,
That darkness will fade with the morning
    and that this will pass away too,
Then nothing in life can defeat me,
    for as long as this knowledge remains,
I can suffer whatever is happening,
    for I know God will break all the chains
That are binding me tight in the darkness
    and trying to fill me with fear,
For there is no night without dawning,
    and I know that my morning is near.

Let's look up and not down. Let's face the storms of doubt
with determination to win. Let's have faith in God and self.
Let's pray. Come on, let's live!

Everett Wentworth Hill

While in the Hospital

How little we know what God has in store
As daily He blesses our lives more and more.
I've lived many years and I've learned many things,
But today I have grown new spiritual wings,
For pain has a way of broadening our view
And bringing us closer in sympathy too,
To those who are living in constant pain
And trying somehow to bravely sustain
The faith and endurance to keep on trying
When they almost welcome the peace of dying.
Without this experience I would have lived and died
Without fathoming the pain of Christ crucified,
For none of us knows what pain's all about
Until our spiritual wings start to sprout.
So thank You, God, for the gift You sent
To teach me that pain is heaven-sent.

The pessimist sees the difficulty in every opportunity; the
optimist, the opportunity in every difficulty.

L. P. Jacks

Reach Out

If your heart needs a lift
  and your spirits are low,
If your outlook is dreary
  and life's lost its glow,
Just reach out to help someone
  and you're sure to find
That most of our unhappiness
  is just a state of mind.

All the beautiful sentiments in the world weigh less than
a single lovely action.

James Russell Lowell

Seasons of Life

We know we must pass
   through the seasons God sends
Content in the knowledge
   that everything ends,
And, oh, what a blessing
   to know there are reasons
And to find that our souls
   must too have their seasons—
Bounteous seasons
   and barren ones too,
Times for rejoicing
   and times to be blue—
But meeting these seasons
   of dark desolation,
With the strength that is born
   of anticipation,

Comes from knowing
　　that every season of sadness
Will surely be followed
　　by a springtime of gladness.

What life means to us is determined not so much by what
life brings to us as the attitude we bring to life; not so
much by what happens to us as by our reaction to what
happens.

Lewis L. Dunnington

Keep Shining

You are someone it is a pleasure to know,
For like a candle's cozy glow,
You brighten and lighten many days
With your sunny smile and cheerful ways.
So keep on shining for many years
In this old world of trials and tears.

Give me a sense of humor, Lord, give me the grace to see
a joke, to get some happiness from life and pass it on to
other folk.

Chester Cathedral

You Are Extra Special

Like a tutti-frutti sundae,
   like a multimillionaire,
Like a double-feature movie,
   like a car with class to spare,
Like a twenty-carat diamond,
   just as brilliant as can be,
You are extra special
   in the way you rate with me.

Age is opportunity no less than youth itself, though in another dress.

Henry Wadsworth Longfellow

Wear a Grin

When your axle is a-draggin
   and your tires are wearin' thin,
Then birthdays are not something
   you welcome with a grin.
And I'm speaking from experience,
   although it's sad but true,
Father Time and Mother Nature
   sure can make it tough for you.
I'll admit I'm getting mildewed
   and my carburetor's busted.
My chassis's cracked and dented,
   and my spark plugs all are rusted.
But what's the use of griping
   because you've stripped your gears,
You can't expect to feel like twenty
   when you've lived over fifty years.

There is one consolation
　　that dries away my tears—
Father Time is after everyone
　　as they travel through the years.
And all the nicest folks I know,
　　including folks like you,
Keep right on having birthdays
　　and growing older too.
But some folks just grow older,
　　but of you that isn't true,
For every time you add a year
　　you grow much nicer too.

The sense of humor is the oil of life's engine. Without it, the machinery creaks and groans. No lot is so hard, no aspect of things so grim, but it relaxes before a hearty laugh.

G. S. Merriam

Forgiveness and Kindness

I often wonder why people do not make more of the marvelous power there is in kindness. It is the greatest lever to move the hearts of humans that the world has ever known—greater far than anything that mere ingenuity can devise or subtlety suggest. Kindness is the kingpin of success in life; it is the prime factor in overcoming friction and making the human machinery run smoothly.

Andrew Chapman

- Be a living example of patience, compassion, faith, and kindness.
- Overlook your neighbor's faltering way of walking, repetitious manner of talking, and difficulty in hearing.
- Stop, linger, smile, and chat a while with a neighbor.
- Offer to help someone learn a skill or talent in which you excel.
- Participate in conversations, but also be a good listener.
- Forgive and forget any slight or hurt directed at you.

More of Thee . . . Less of Me

Take me and break me and make me, dear God,
   just what You want me to be.
Give me the strength to accept what you send
   and eyes with the vision to see
All the small arrogant ways that I have
   and the vain little things that I do,
Make me aware that I'm often concerned
   more with myself than with You.
Uncover before me my weakness and greed
   and help me to search deep inside,
So I may discover how easy it is
   to be selfishly lost in my pride.

And then in Thy goodness and mercy
   look down on this weak, erring one
And tell me that I am forgiven
   for all I've so willingly done.

If I have learned anything in the swift unrolling of the
web of time, it is the virtue of tolerance, of moderation in
thought and deed, of forbearance toward one's fellow
men and women.

A. J. Cronin

Forgive Us

Bless us, heavenly Father,
   forgive our erring ways,
Grant us strength to serve You,
   put purpose in our days.
Give us understanding,
   enough to make us kind,
So we may judge all people
   with our hearts and not our minds.
And teach us to be patient
   in everything we do,
Content to trust Your wisdom
   and to follow after You.
And help us when we falter,
   and hear us when we pray,
And receive us in Your kingdom
   to dwell with You some day.

To err is human, to forgive, divine.

Alexander Pope

To Really Live

Since God forgives us,
   we too must forgive
And resolve to do better
   each day that we live,
By constantly trying
   to be like Him more nearly
And to trust in His wisdom
   and to love Him more dearly.

Father, hallowed be your name, your kingdom come. Give
us each day our daily bread. Forgive us our sins, for we
also forgive everyone who sins against us.

Luke 11:2–4 NIV

Each Life Has a Purpose

Everyone has his or her own little niche,
   no matter how tiny or small,
For every life has a purpose
   or we wouldn't be here at all.
For there is no one here on earth
   who hasn't a part to play,
Some little thing to contribute,
   something to do or to say,
Some way to be useful to someone,
   no matter how small the deed,
Some way to be helpful to others—
   those who are deep in need.

I am only one, but still I am one; I cannot do everything, but still I can do something; and because I cannot do everything I will not refuse to do something that I can do.

Edward Everett Hale

Time to Be Kind

In this busy world
  it's refreshing to find
People who still have
  the time to be kind,
People still ready—
  by thought, word, or deed—
To reach out a hand
  in an hour of need,
People who still have
  the faith to believe
That the more you give,
  the more you receive.

To stand strong graciously; to smile sincerely; to love always; and to seek understanding—these are the worthy ambitions of a life worth living.

Esther Freshman

Life Is Worth Living

God, grant us a wider view
So we see others' faults through the eyes of You.
Teach us to judge not with hasty tongue
Neither the old nor the young.
Give us the patience and grace to endure
And a stronger faith so we feel secure,
And instead of remembering, help us forget
The irritations that caused us to fret—
Freely forgiving for some offense
And finding each day a rich recompense
In offering a friendly, helping hand
And trying in all ways to understand
That all of us, whoever we are,
Are trying to reach an unreachable star.
For the great and small, the good and bad,
The young and old, the sad and glad
Are asking today, "Is life worth living?"
And the answer is only in loving and giving,
For only love can make us kind,
And kindness of heart brings peace of mind.

The world is a looking glass and gives back to every person the reflection of his or her own face. Frown at it, and it in turn will look sourly at you; laugh at it, and with it, and it is a jolly, kind companion.

William Makepeace Thackeray

Favorite Memories

One of the most precious of human faculties is memory. Youth thinks of it only as an aid to learning and advancement. But as the years roll on, it becomes a treasure storehouse. The highlights of all the years are there—vivid pictures of beauties appreciated, heartwarming reminiscences of friends we've known, tender thoughts of family mingled with gratitude for their understanding through the years, the satisfaction of recalling work well done, a feeling that we have meant something to those who meant so much to us—highlights stored in memory's treasure house to be recalled at will to encourage and sustain us whenever we need them.

Nuggets

- Send a note or call to congratulate a friend for a special happening.
- Create a memory album with old photographs and fond memorabilia.
- Watch family movies or family videos with your loved ones.
- Teach a game or a card trick to a youngster.
- Write a poem or paragraph about yourself. Include information you desire others to always remember about you.
- Celebrate your birthdays. Have a cake and always "add a candle to grow on."

Priceless Treasure

I've many pleasant memories
  of little things you've done,
Not just for me but all the others
  for you helped out everyone.
And great must be your happiness
  and your satisfaction too
In looking back and knowing
  you did all that you could do
To help the one beside you—
  you gave your best full measure—
And that is one thing
  that is a priceless treasure.
For there's no richer blessing
  than to go to sleep at night
Secure in the sweet knowledge
  that you treated others right.

The most consummately beautiful thing in the universe
is the rightly fashioned life of a good person.

George Herbert Palmer

Memories

May heartwarming memories of old times and places
Bring joy to your hearts and smiles to your faces
As you look back across the years that have fled
And remember together the day you were wed.
So much has happened and so much has changed
Since the day your vows were lovingly exchanged,
But in spite of change one thing remains true,
You've kept your hearts young and your love new.
And this brings you good wishes and also a prayer
That both of you will continue to share
The deep golden beauty of life's autumn of love
As each day is blessed by the Lord up above.

No man or woman knows what perfect love is, until they
have been married a quarter of a century.

Mark Twain

Remembrance Road

There's a road I call remembrance
   where I walk each day with you.
It's a pleasant, happy road, my dear,
   all filled with memories true.
Today it leads me through a spot
   where I can dream a while,
And in its tranquil peacefulness
   I touch your hand and smile.
There are hills and fields and budding trees
   and stillness that's so sweet
That it seems that this must be the place
   where God and humans meet.

I hope we can go back again
   and golden hours renew,
And may God be with you always,
   until the day we do.

Of all the music that reached farthest into heaven, it is the
beating of a loving heart.

Henry Ward Beecher

A Wonderful Occasion

What a wonderful occasion and what a rare one too,
No wonder your friends are so happy for you.
And I just want to join with the many who say,
May this be a perfectly wonderful day.
Through fifty years your love has grown dearer,
And each anniversary has made it much clearer
That love is much more than a tender caress
And more than bright hours of sheer happiness.
You're a perfect example of what marriage should be
And a great inspiration for the whole world to see,
And the world would be better and luckier by far
If all married couples were the kind that you are.

Gray hair is a crown of splendor;
it is attained by a righteous life.

Proverbs 16:31 NIV

Listen with Your Heart

Memories are treasures
   time cannot take away,
So may you be surrounded
   by happy ones today.
May all the love and tenderness
   of golden years well spent
Come back today to fill your heart
   with beauty and content.

I love thee with the breath, smiles, tears of all my life!—
and if God choose, I shall but love thee better after death.

Elizabeth Barrett Browning

Life's Golden Autumn

Birthdays come and birthdays go,
   and with them comes the thought
Of all the happy memories
   the passing years have brought.
And looking back across the years
   it's a joy to reminisce,
For memory opens wide the door
   on a happy day like this.
And with a sweet nostalgia
   we longingly recall
The happy days of long ago
   that seem the best of all.

But time cannot be halted
　　in its swift and endless flight,
And age is sure to follow youth
　　as day comes after night.
But while our steps grow slower
　　and we grow more tired too,
The soul goes roaring upward
　　to realms untouched and new.

I believe that a man is as young as his mind. It is not the
passing years, but the loss of enthusiasm for the adventure of living that wrinkles the soul. A man is as old as his
doubt, as young as his faith. I believe in the future; the
past was great and I believe the future will be greater.

Author Unknown

Fulfillment in Retirement

Think of what the world would have missed had a retirement age, even of 70 years, been universally enforced.

Gladstone was Prime Minister of England at 83; Benjamin Franklin helped frame the Constitution of the United States at 80; Oliver Wendell Holmes retired from the Supreme Court Bench at 91; Henry Ford, past age 80, took up the presidency of the Ford Motor Company for the second time after his son's death; Amos Alonzo Stagg was named the "Football Man of the Year" at 81.

Wingate M. Johnson

- Look forward not backward. Retirement age offers new opportunities with fewer responsibilities.
- Keep a youthful spirit. The future can be filled with zest.
- Observe safety precautions to minimize accidents. Use contrasting colors on floors to indicate steps or elevations between rooms. Install carbon monoxide and smoke detectors near your bedroom.
- Learn something you always wanted to but never had the opportunity to learn: a foreign language, a skill, or how to play a musical instrument.
- Investigate programs and benefits available to mature individuals.
- Keep your legal and financial affairs updated.
- Use your experience, knowledge, talent, and time in a volunteer situation. Retirees are a valuable resource.
- Participate in mission work or other services for the Lord.
- Take a trip or sign up for a class. The International Elderhostel, which sponors travel and educational courses for mature adults, is located in Boston, Massachusetts.

Show Me

Lord, show me the way I can somehow repay
   the blessings You've given to me.
Lord, teach me to do what you most want me to
   and to be what You want me to be.

A nationwide survey of new activities by states and public agencies for the aged shows educators agree that learning knows no limits.

Thomas C. Desmond

Returning Home

It's nice to travel far and wide
  and view God's endless splendor,
But there is something wonderful
  and infinitely more tender
To come back home and realize
  that only by God's grace
Could we have traveled safely
  as we went from place to place.
And what a privilege it is
  to lift our hearts above
In thanks to Him who brought us back
  to our home and those we love.

It will be great to go up to the moon. But earth never invented anything better than coming home—provided home is a center of affection where parents love each other and their children intelligently, and where children admire and respect their parents and want to grow up to be like them.

Author Unknown

The Joy of Unselfish Giving

Time is not measured by the years you live
But by the deeds you do and the joy you give,
And from year to year the good Lord above
Bestows on His children the gift of His love,
Asking us only to share it with others
By treating all people not as strangers but brothers.
Each day as it comes brings a chance to each one
To love to the fullest, leaving nothing undone
That would brighten the life or lighten the load
Of some weary traveler lost on life's road.
So what does it matter how long we may live
If as long as we live we unselfishly give.

The value of service lies in the spirit in which you serve
and not in the importance or magnitude of the service.
Even the lowliest task or deed is made holy, joyous, and
prosperous when it is filled with love.

Charles Fillmore

Why are we living?
  What can we do?
How can we help
  and be happy too?
Why are we here?
  What are our goals?
Are we creatures of body
  or saints with souls?
How can we discover
  the fullness of living?
How?
  By experiencing the joy of giving!

No one grows old by living—only by losing interest in living.

Marie Ray

New Dimensions

Here's hoping your retirement
  will turn out to be for you
A time of new beginnings
  and new dimensions too.
And may the happy satisfaction
  of a splendid job well done
Help to make your earned retirement
  a very pleasant one
In which you find fulfillment
  of your creative art
And joy in every avenue
  of spirit, mind, and heart.

Those who face the issue of retirement squarely, and cross the barrier by decisive action . . . enter at once into a new and wonderful promised land. Preparation for the full use of the dividend years is a by-product of the intelligent employment of all the years. Just as prudence requires that out of each pay check something be set aside to meet the economic necessities of the senior period, so later contentment requires that in each working year some new talent be developed, some new interest cultivated, that looks to the future for fulfillment.

Clarence B. Randall

Sharing Wisdom

The years go by
  and as they do
They only pause
  to smile on you,
For you hold together
  in happy thought
All the richness that
  this life has brought,
And you give so freely
  to all you meet
The wisdom that makes
  your life complete.
And you'll never grow old
  for you've so much to give,
And you'll always be young
  for you've learned how to live.

If you have knowledge, let others light their candles at it.

Thomas Fuller

Time for Everything

A time to laugh, a time to cry.
A time to live, a time to die.
A time to sow, a time to reap.
A time to sing, a time to weep.
A time to work, a time to play.
A time to go, a time to stay.
Why can't we learn this ageless truth
So when we lose our springtime youth
We gallantly accept our years
Without resentment, fears, or tears?
Why can't we just thank God and say
We know that all things pass away?

For God's wisdom, love, and grace
Ordained these changes to take place,
And we can never change God's plan,
For God still knows what's best for man.

For everything there is a season, and a time for every matter under heaven.

Ecclesiastes 3:1 RSV

Another Year Closer to God

Your many years of loving God
   have been golden years well spent,
Which have brought a golden harvest
   of deep, serene content.
For glorious is the gladness
   and rich is the reward
Of all who work unceasingly
   in the service of the Lord.
And I know our heavenly Father
   has directed you each day
As you try to serve and please Him,
   as you follow in His way.
And looking back across your life,
   your spirit grows serene,
As your soul in love envisions
   what your eyes have never seen.

And while the springtime of your life
   is pleasant to recall,
You know the autumn of life
   is the richest time of all,
For great has been your gladness
   and priceless your reward
As through the years you walked with joy
   in the vineyard of the Lord.
For to know God and to serve Him
   is a joy beyond all price,
And no one knows this better
   than Helen Steiner Rice.

I have received much kindness from men and numberless mercies from God. Those kindnesses I can only return to my fellow men; and I can only show my gratitude for these mercies from God by my readiness to help my brethren.

Benjamin Franklin

The Big Move

I have thought of you so often and so much since your letter arrived telling me you were preparing to move. I did not write immediately because I know so well how very upsetting and confusing things are when we are in the process of making such a very gigantic change.

It is always so disturbing to our emotions when we have to tear ourselves away from treasured associations and old familiar surroundings, but after you have made the adjustments, you will be very happy—I know—and I am so glad you were wise enough to make the change while you could still do it with planned leisure and before it became a necessity. I find, as we grow older, we all have far less energy and endurance, and it is the very wise who know how to conserve what they have to expend on the things that are nearest and dearest to their hearts. . . .

When you're comfortably settled
    in your home so nice and new,
May you find good luck and friendship
    have moved right in with you,
Making every moment happy,
    adding joy to every day,
Bringing never ending pleasure
    more than words can ever say.

I think you know that you are taking all my good wishes with you into your new residence, and I know that it will be a place where God and love abide, for I think we both realize that . . .

It's not the tables, nor the chairs,
　　nor the pictures on the wall,
That fill a home with happiness—
　　it's not those things at all—
But loving hearts and friendly smiles,
　　and faith that's strong and true,
And may these blessings bring real joy
　　to your new home—and you.

Grow old along with me, the best is yet to be.

Robert Browning

Emergency Help Guide

You may never need an emergency help guide, but create one—just in case. Include information such as:

Full name _____

Date of birth _____

Social security number _____

Medicaid number _____

Medicare number _____

Health insurance policy _____

Other insurance policies _____

_____

Names and numbers of those to contact in case of an
emergency _____

_____

_____

Choice of hospital _____

_____

Doctor's name and telephone number_____

_____

Health history_____

_____

_____

_____

Present health problems _____

_____

_____

_____

_____

Medications, prescribed and over-the-counter, used
regularly _____

_____

_____

Names and numbers of

Family members _____

_____

_____

_____

_____

_____

Church and pastor _____

_____

Attorney _____

_____

Pharmacist _____

_____

God's Unfailing Promise

From one day to another
  God will gladly give
To everyone who seeks Him
  and tries each day to live
A little bit more closely
  to God and to each other
Seeing everyone who passes
  as a neighbor, friend, or brother,
Not only joy and happiness
  but the faith to meet each trial
Not with trepidation
  but with an inner smile
And the knowledge that life's measured
  not by how many years we live
But by the kindly things we do
  and the happiness we give.